Preface:

Dear Reader,

"The Workbook – Entrepreneurship at your doorstep – Today & Everyday" was conceived when I was searching for answers to certain questions lingering in my mind from my professional career and from the initial days of my Entrepreneurial debut.

I created this Workbook so that I could answer the questions that came in my mind. This was done through well-structured exercises revolving around Entrepreneurship.

I finished the exercises of this Workbook and found myself more confident in going forward with my "startup venture". This Workbook will help you firm up your mind in starting on your own. On the other hand, even if you don't want to start your own, still this Workbook will be of great help to you for developing an entrepreneurial attitude at your workplace.

As this is a Workbook which I have completed myself, I would be available to guide the readers through the exercises mentioned in this Workbook.

You can reach me at sanjaynair005@gmail.com for any queries or guidance required for completing this Workbook.

With Best Wishes and Regards,

Sanjay Nair

About the Author:

Sanjay Nair is a Professional Consultant with more than 16 years of Experience in the field of Marketing and Commercialization. After working with reputed companies Nationally and Internationally, Sanjay Nair now runs his own Consulting firm in Hyderabad, India.

You can reach Sanjay Nair at his email id: sanjaynair005@gmail.com

Contents:

Entrepreneurship at your doorstep - Today and Everyday

Introduction:

"Entrepreneurship at your doorstep – Today and Everyday" is a Workbook which intends to ignite the latent Entrepreneurial spirit that is present in many of us. Through a series of exercises this workbook will explore your creative ideas and bring it to the forefront so that you can monetize them by proper execution.

I. **You are on your own:**

Entrepreneurship is an exciting path but many times it is a lonely path as well. You must handle multiple roles when you become an entrepreneur. You become the leader, you become the follower and you become the doer as well. In essence you are on your own. You have to keep motivating yourself every day and in fact every hour. The entrepreneurial attitude demands much more than the normal. It demands to unleash your wild animal spirit in the Jungle out there. Do you have it in you? The following exercise is a good way to start thinking on those lines.

Exercise 1: Make Notes on the bellow mentioned points and ascertain whether you are ready to unleash your entrepreneurial spirit?

1. Identify your Passion and get in sync with it.
2. Are you ready to ride your Passion? If yes question how it can be done differently?
3. Branch out all possibilities – And thereafter Synchronize to deduce feasible alternatives
4. Be ready to take calculated risks – What are those risks that you can take?
5. Keep a timeline and go for Execution.

II. **Don't kill your ideas yourself:**

Most of the times we are the worst critics of our own ideas and we kill it ourselves. How many times we got a terrific insight but because of not going into the details or because of not following up "the insight" with concrete measures, we kill it ourselves by thinking on a defeatist line latter on. An entrepreneurial attitude demands monetizing of our ideas and insights that we get. Let's do an exercise which will help us streamline our ideas and measure our ideas on its monetizing potential.

Exercise 2: Create a Note based on the bellow 5 points and take one step forward to Monetize your Wild ideas.

1. Jump at it - Even if you have not ascertained the whole picture
2. Count on experiences – Good and Bad and keep moving forward
3. Explore the unexplored – Go where you have never gone before
4. Let your creative juice flow out
5. Fly high but be grounded as well – Give a structure and plan to your wild ideas

III. Work zealously to fructify your ideas:

Having ideas is one thing but converting those ideas and insights into actual work plans which can be monetized is all together a different ball game. An entrepreneurial attitude requires converting your ideas into effective work plans and thereafter zealously implementing or executing those work plans. The following exercise will help you to get into execution mode.

Exercise 3: Make a one-page Document from the bellow 6 points to take forward the Journey from a Creative Idea to Execution

1. Summary – A paragraph on all the bellow once you have written it
2. Purpose – Why and What?
3. Audience – For Whom?
4. Execution – What is The Roadmap?
5. Timeline –What Timeframe?
6. Conclusion - What would be the Path forward?

IV. Step towards developing an entrepreneurial mindset and some case studies:

An entrepreneurial attitude is a hunter's attitude. It demands sharp observational skills to grab ideas and insights from the environment and convert them into work plans which can be properly executed and monetized. An entrepreneurial attitude requires rising the antenna of all your senses to hyper mode and continuously hunting for ideas and insights that can be eventually monetized. Let's analyze the following case studies and carryout an exercise to sharpen our entrepreneurial mindset.

Exercise 4: Study the bellow mentioned 12 great entrepreneurs of our time and understand how one can develop an Entrepreneurial attitude

1. Steve Jobs
2. Bill Gates
3. Fred Smith
4. Jeff Bezos
5. Larry Page and Sergey Brin

6. Howard Schultz
7. Mark Zuckerberg
8. John Mackey
9. Herb Kelleher
10. N.R. Narayana Murthy
11. Sam Walton
12. Muhammad Yunus

V. Starting on your own:

Starting on your own is a natural progression of an Entrepreneurial attitude. That great thought that you had 20 years back also can trigger you to start your own. It's the timing that's the most important as well as that feeling that now you are ready for it. Let's do an exercise and see if you are ready for it?

Exercise 5: If you are finally decided to start your own, then it's time to get into the Nitty-gritty. Carry out the bellow mentioned activities to further hasten the process.

1. Make Sure Entrepreneurship Is What You Really Want
2. Decide What Kind of Business You Want
3. Research Your Idea
4. Write a Business Plan

VI. Help you need from Others and help you don't need from Others:

Once you decide to start your own, it's important to understand that you would be needing help from a set of people and you won't be needing help from another set of people. Success stories are always projected out there in the environment through multiple media but what you need is the company of people in entrepreneurial action. By association with these set of people you get hands on experience on what must be done and what's that should not be done. Taking help from these people will hasten your learning curve. On the other hand, approaching established players will only give you a perspective of what they did once upon a time to be successful. That's not real-time action on any account. Moreover, your Partners, Employees, Friends, and Family will also play a key role in the success of your entrepreneurial debut.

Let's do an exercise to identify people with whom you would like to associate with.

Exercise 6: Identify Mentors, Partners, potential Employees as well as Friends and Family members from whom you would be needing support for your Entrepreneurial Debut.

1. Have Mentors who are in thick of action themselves. This way the learning curve will be faster.
2. Choose Partners with whom you can develop a working relationship
3. Select Employees who can run the business along with you
4. Involve Friends you make time for - It's even better if these friends are themselves involved in some kind entrepreneurial activities.
5. And Get at least some Key members in the Family to support you

VII. Entrepreneurial environment - Where to find what?

Most importantly we should know "where to find what" if finally, we decide to start our own. How we are going to register our startup enterprise? Who are going to collaborate with us? Who would be funding our enterprise? What would be our goals? What would be our products or services? Who would be our customers? Who would be our Vendors? All these questions need to be properly defined through a Business plan.

Let's do an exercise to develop a Business plan.

Exercise 7: Now it's time to write your Business plan which needs to cover the Executive Summary, Business/Industry Overview, **Market Analysis and the Competition**, Sales and Marketing Plan, Ownership and Management Plan, Operating Plan, and most importantly sound Financial plan.

1. Executive Summary – To be written at the end
2. Business/Industry Overview – Is the Industry growing? Is it booming?
3. Market Analysis and the Competition – Who are the Direct and Indirect Competitors?
4. Sales and Marketing Plan – What numbers you plan to achieve and for that what kind of Marketing spend that you are going to allocate?
5. Ownership and Management Plan – Would you go Solo or with partners?
6. Operating Plan – What are the things you are going to do in a financial year to achieve your numbers (Sales plan)
7. Financial Plan – Where from the Money will come and how you are going to allocate it and how you are expecting the returns to come?

Conclusion:

An entrepreneurial attitude is a habit, so cultivate it anyways

WORKBOOK EXERCISE SPACE:

www.ingramcontent.com/pod-product-compliance
Lightning Source LLC
Chambersburg PA
CBHW070935220526
45468CB00005B/1779